BASIC SKILLS
FOR THE
NEW ARBITRATOR

Second Edition

Books by Allan H. Goodman

Basic Skills for the New Mediator

Basic Skills for the New Arbitrator

BASIC SKILLS
FOR THE
NEW ARBITRATOR
Second Edition

ALLAN H. GOODMAN

SOLOMON PUBLICATIONS

Basic Skills for the New Arbitrator, Second Edition
© Copyright 2004 by Allan H. Goodman

All images inside this book © Copyright www.arttoday.com

Printed in the United States of America

First Printing, Second Edition   May 2004

Published and Distributed in the United States and Canada by:

Solomon Publications
PO Box 2124 Rockville, MD 20847-2124
(301) 816-1025
book@solomonpublications.com
www.solomonpublications.com

Library of Congress Catalog Number 2004092925

ISBN 0-9670973-2-0

About the Author

Allan H. Goodman is a private arbitrator and mediator. He is also an arbitrator and mediator trainer and the author of the companion volume BASIC SKILLS FOR THE NEW MEDIATOR.

He is a graduate of the Georgetown University School of Foreign Service and the University of Toledo College of Law and is a member of the bars of District of Columbia, Maryland, and Virginia.

From 1975 to 1993 he was an attorney in private practice. He is currently a Judge on the United States General Services Administration Board of Contract Appeals.

Brief Table of Contents

Contents

INTRODUCTION TO THE SECOND EDITION

I wrote **Basic Skills for the New Arbitrator** ten years ago, after serving as a private arbitrator in approximately fifty cases. I have continued to practice as a private arbitrator and arbitrator trainer. I have added to my knowledge of the arbitration process by serving in increasingly complex cases, working with fellow arbitrators, and hearing the experiences of those I have trained.

The first edition of this book has been extremely well received, and I have benefited from many comments and questions from readers. The increase in the use of alternative dispute resolution techniques has sparked a tremendous interest among attorneys and other professionals to serve as arbitrators in their fields of expertise.

It is now time to issue a second edition to share my additional experiences and those of my colleagues and readers. Many have suggested that a topic index would be helpful, in addition to the detailed table of contents listing the 100 questions. I have therefore included a topic index in the back of the book.

INTRODUCTION TO THE FIRST EDITION

Arbitration is an alternative to resolving disputes in court. The arbitration process allows the parties to select an individual or several individuals with expertise in the subject matter of the dispute to listen to the evidence and render a binding decision.

After ten years as a practicing attorney, I yearned for an opportunity to actually decide a case rather than advocating the position of one of the parties. Serving as an arbitrator allowed me to fulfill my desire to resolve disputes.

Since my first appointment as an arbitrator, I have served in many cases administered through various arbitration organizations. In these instances, I have had the benefit of rules and procedures previously established by the administering organizations. I also have served as an arbitrator in cases that I administered myself, during which I and the parties have had to devise our own procedures and methods for resolving the matter in dispute.

While there are many published court decisions which deal with legal issues arising from arbitration, I have found that these decisions often offer little practical guidance to the arbitrator as to how to conduct an arbitration proceeding. The practical guidance that I have received has come from fellow arbitrators and personnel from the various arbitration organizations with whom I have worked.

Over the years, I learned by doing and consulting with other arbitrators. I followed my instincts, reacted to situations, and refined my techniques. As an arbitrator, I have found a great deal of personal satisfaction in dispute resolution.

This book contains my answers to one hundred questions a new arbitrator might ask concerning the arbitration process and the role of the arbitrator. It is not meant to instruct attorneys how to represent clients in arbitration, nor does it contain instruction for serving as a mediator, which is a different technique for resolving disputes.

My answers reflect my experience and opinion, and are not meant to be definitive. Your experience may differ from mine. Please note that Question No. 101 is your question to ask me. I also welcome any other suggestions or comments.

THE MYTH AND REALITY OF ARBITRATION

The King gave the order, "Fetch me a sword."
A sword was brought before the King and
the King said, "Cut the live child in two,
and give half to one and half to the other." I Kings 3:24-25

There is a **myth** about arbitration. As an attorney, I heard it from clients and fellow attorneys. I did not have personal experience that the myth was probably not true until I rendered my first arbitration award. Yet, the myth persists, usually in the following form:

Arbitration? That's when you don't go to court, but pick somebody to decide the case informally. You have a hearing in front of the arbitrator and the arbitrator will usually "split the baby" - you know, give you at least half of what you ask for.

This myth is not only factually inaccurate as it applies to arbitration today, but it is historically inaccurate as to the original dispute to which it refers. The story of King Solomon's first arbitration does not support the arbitration myth. Let us first consider testimony of the witnesses.

Two women came before the King. The first woman said "This woman and I live in the same house. I gave birth to a child and she gave birth to a child. During the night, her child died. She arose in the night and took my child, and laid her dead child on me. When I awoke to nurse my child, he was dead, but when I looked at him closely he was not my child." The other woman spoke. "No, the live one is my son, and the dead one is yours." But the first insisted, "No the dead boy is yours; mine is the live one." And they went on arguing before the King.

15

At this point, King Solomon rendered an interim award.

"Fetch me a sword." A sword was brought before the King and the King said, "Cut the live child in two, and give half to one and half to the other."

In response, one of the parties requested modification of the award.

But one of the women pleaded with the King, "Give the live child to her, only do not kill it." The other insisted, "It shall be neither yours nor mine, cut it in two."

Faced with this additional testimony, King Solomon modified his award.

Then the King spoke, "Give the live child to the one who pleaded for its life - and do not put it to death; she is its mother."

It is important to note what King Solomon did *not* do. *He did not split the baby!*

What then is the **reality** of arbitration? From the arbitrator's perspective, my personal experience is that in rendering an arbitration award, I do not "split the baby." In fact, I have never been tempted to do so. The parties' goal is not a simplistic 50%-50% compromise solution, or else they would have settled the matter themselves. If they do wish to compromise, they still may do so at any time after arbitration is initiated.

The parties must meet a burden of proof in arbitration, just as they must in litigation. Even if a party proves entitlement to damages, the amount of damages still must be proved, based upon evidence presented. The entitlement to damages and the amount of damages must be based upon proof, not an arbitrary split of the amounts claimed. If I grant a claim substantially in full, or almost in full, or deny a claim in its entirety, it is because the party has either met or failed to meet the burden of proof. I do not reward a claimant half of its claim for just "spending the time."

The reality of arbitration from the parties' perspective is that *the parties will always know more about the dispute than an arbitrator ever will.* They have lived with the situation until it evolved into a dispute. Even when the time arrives to make an award, the arbitrator may still know less than the parties know. In any situation involving advocacy, the trier of fact is left with the "spin" that the parties place on the facts. Even so, if the arbitrator has performed the duties of the position well, and taken appropriate steps to control the process so that the necessary information is submitted by the parties, the arbitrator can arrive at a reasoned, supportable decision.

Your function as an arbitrator is not to give a party to the arbitration an "A" for effort, anger or indignation. Your compassion for the situations presented to you must be tempered with objectivity. Your responsibility is to render an award based on the evidence. When Solomon became king, he realized the difficulty of the decisions he would be required to make. His fervent prayer was for an "understanding heart."

GLOSSARY

Arbitration is the process in which parties to a dispute agree to submit the dispute to a third party, known as an arbitrator, and confer upon the arbitrator the authority to review the evidence and render a decision.

The party requesting relief in arbitration is the **claimant**.

The claimant initiates arbitration by filing an **arbitration demand**, a statement that contains the basis and amount of its claim.

The party against whom the arbitration demand is made is known as the **respondent.** The respondent may defend against the claimant's claim, by filing an **answer** to the demand, and the respondent may also have its own claim against the claimant. If the respondent has its own claim, it files a **counterclaim**.

The parties may designate an **administering organization** to administer the arbitration. The arbitration demand is filed with the administering organization, and an individual known as a **case administrator** is responsible for aiding the parties in choosing the arbitrator from the list maintained by the administering organization and acts as the liaison among the claimant, respondent, and the arbitrator.

If an administering organization is not used, the parties themselves will choose the arbitrator. The arbitrator will communicate with the parties without the intermediary of the administering organization and the case administrator, being careful not to have *ex parte* communication with any party. *Ex parte* communication is communication with one party without the other party present.

In complex cases, more than one arbitrator may be requested by the parties, and a **panel** of arbitrators is appointed. Usually, an arbitration panel consists of three members, one of whom is designated the **chairperson of the panel.**

The arbitrator's decision is called an **award.** If the parties have entered into **binding arbitration**, in which they agree in advance to abide by the arbitrator's award, a prevailing party may go to court and seek to **enforce** an award if the non-prevailing party does not abide by the terms and conditions of the award.

A non-prevailing party that is dissatisfied with an award may request a court to **vacate** the award under certain circumstances.

ONE HUNDRED QUESTIONS AND ANSWERS

The one hundred questions in this book are those questions that new arbitrators have asked most frequently during training sessions.

This book is written for both the attorney and non-attorney arbitrator. Some of the questions and answers deal with basic principles of procedure and evidence that may already be apparent to the attorney arbitrator. I recommend that the readers who are attorneys review these portions on procedure and evidence, despite their familiarity with the principles discussed, as the discussion is written from the perspective of the arbitrator, rather than the more familiar viewpoint of the advocate.

I wrote this book so that you can read it from start to finish, and also as a reference, if you are in the middle of a hearing and need a quick answer. The answers to many of the questions are my opinions. You may be able to offer a more complete or creative answer, and if so I welcome the opportunity to share your comments. Please write to me at the address provided at the end of the book.

Questions are arranged in the chronological order of the arbitration process. In **THE ARBITRATION PROCESS AND ROLE OF THE ARBITRATOR**, we discuss the general concepts of arbitration and the arbitrator's role, including the arbitrator's duty of disclosure. **PREHEARING PROCEDURES AND THE PRELIMINARY CONFERENCE** contains detailed instruction on prehearing management, and focuses on the preliminary conference as a procedural means to assure that the parties effectively prepare for the hearing. Prehearing management after the preliminary conference is further explored in **PREHEARING SUBMISSIONS, SUBPOENAS, AND DISCOVERY DISPUTES.**

The majority of the questions, as you would expect, are contained in **CONDUCTING THE HEARING**. I discuss handling common delay tactics, choosing the physical facilities required for the hearing, avoiding improper contact with the parties, allowing witnesses to remain in the hearing room, responding to objections, dealing with hostile individuals, and many other topics.

In **THE ARBITRATION AWARD** and **AFTER THE AWARD**, guidelines are included for drafting the award and the requirements as to arbitrator conduct after the award is transmitted to the parties. Tips on arranging for compensation are included in **GETTING PAID**. Finally, the **CONCLUSION** sets forth what I believe is the fundamental principle of being an arbitrator.

The Arbitration Process and the Role of the Arbitrator

THE ARBITRATION PROCESS AND
THE ROLE OF THE ARBITRATOR

1. What is the difference between binding and nonbinding arbitration?

Arbitration is the process by which parties to a dispute appoint a person known as the arbitrator to listen to the evidence and render a decision as to which party will prevail. In **binding arbitration**, the parties agree to abide by the decision of the arbitrator, just as they would abide by the decision of a judge or a jury in court. This book deals with binding arbitration.

There is a process known as **nonbinding arbitration**, in which the parties agree that they need not be bound by the arbitrator's decision. They use the arbitration process to obtain an advisory opinion from the arbitrator. In nonbinding arbitration, the parties may ultimately decide to abide by an arbitrator's decision, if they have confidence in the arbitrator's decision and a desire to resolve the dispute without resorting to costly litigation.

2. What is the difference between arbitration and mediation?

In your capacity as an arbitrator, the parties to the dispute confer upon you the authority to hear the evidence they present and then render an award. You decide the outcome of the dispute. They present the evidence during a hearing, by bringing witnesses with actual knowledge of the events, and you consider the evidence and decide which party will prevail.

In contrast to the authority of an arbitrator, a mediator has no authority to render an award, and does not decide the outcome of the dispute. Instead, the mediator works with the parties to explore the strengths and weaknesses of their cases, and attempts to have the parties reach a mutually agreeable settlement. In so doing, the mediator does not necessarily review in detail the evidence pertinent to the dispute, as an arbitrator would do, nor does the mediator decide which party should prevail. The mediator acts as a facilitator of the parties' settlement discussions. Sometimes mediation results in a settlement, sometimes it does not. If mediation fails, the next step may be arbitration or litigation.

3. When do parties agree to resolve a dispute by arbitration?

When parties enter into a contract, they will often include an **arbitration clause** in which they agree that any disputes that arise during performance of the contract will be resolved by arbitration. An arbitrator is usually not chosen until a dispute arises, although some contracts require that the parties choose an arbitrator to serve for the duration of the contract while the contract is being performed, even before any disputes arise. A contract clause is not a prerequisite for arbitration. After a dispute arises, the parties may still agree to submit a dispute to arbitration, even if the contract does not contain an arbitration clause.

4. What if a party to an arbitration agreement files a lawsuit?

If a party to an arbitration agreement files a lawsuit, the other party who wants to have the dispute arbitrated may request the court to suspend the lawsuit and compel the other party to arbitrate. Arbitration is favored by the courts, and the courts will usually enforce the parties' agreement to arbitrate. The court usually "stays" or "suspends" the proceedings in court pending the outcome of the arbitration, and may also impose a time period during which the arbitration must be concluded.

If a lawsuit is filed, the party who wants the dispute to be arbitrated must act promptly. If it files an answer to the lawsuit and allows the lawsuit to proceed without promptly requesting that the dispute be arbitrated, the court may not allow the case to be stayed, finding that the party's failure to promptly request a stay has resulted in the waiver of the right to arbitrate.

5. Do I have to be a lawyer in order to serve as an arbitrator?

No. Arbitration began as a means to avoid courts by appointing an individual knowledgeable in a specific industry to resolve a dispute based upon that person's technical knowledge of the subject matter. Contractors, engineers, architects, and real estate developers serve as arbitrators in construction disputes. Stock brokers serve in disputes involving securities fraud and mismanagement. Accountants, computer consultants, and other professionals serve on matters within their realm of expertise.

In recent years, arbitration has taken on the trappings of litigation, with the involvement of lawyers, but the continuing reason for arbitration is to choose those with technical knowledge in the subject matter of the dispute to act as arbitrators. Lawyers are accustomed to dealing with courtroom procedures and examination of witnesses. These techniques are used in arbitration, but in a more informal setting. As an arbitrator, you can learn and employ these procedures to the extent necessary to maintain an orderly presentation in the hearing.

6. Why do some cases need more than one arbitrator?

Some complex cases require a panel of arbitrators. Usually there are three arbitrators on an arbitration panel. A panel offers the parties an opportunity to have individuals of different backgrounds combine their talents. In construction cases, for example, the parties may choose an arbitration panel consisting of a lawyer, a contractor, and an engineer.

The arbitration panel chooses a **chairperson** who serves as the contact between the arbitration panel and the administering organization If there is no administering organization, the chairperson serves as the contact with the parties. The panel can confer ministerial duties upon the chairperson, such as the authority to sign subpoenas for the entire panel, after conferring with the panel. During the hearing, the chairperson rules on objections after conferring with the panel, and serves to direct the hearing procedurally. Of course, the award is the joint decision of the panel members.

7. Are the rules of evidence applied in arbitration?

The rules of evidence are not esoteric principles that exist solely for the benefit of lawyers and judges. We apply the major concepts of the rules of evidence to deal with personal and business situations. There are three basic principles that are the foundation of the rules of evidence - authenticity, relevancy and credibility.

Authenticity is concerned with whether physical evidence is what it purports to be. Was the letter actually written an signed by the person whose signature appears on it? Was the soil sample actually taken from the location indicated?

Relevancy concerns whether or not the evidence tends to prove or disprove a fact that is essential to a party's case. If the evidence presented does not tend to prove or disprove such a fact, there is no reason to consider it.

Credibility is the determination as to whether the evidence is believable. There are varying degrees of credibility. Attorneys sometimes refer to the degree of credibility by stating that the evidence is accorded great or little **weight** by the court or the arbitrator.

You make determinations every day as to authenticity, relevancy and credibility. You probably presume the authenticity of information you receive. When someone attempts to convince you that a fact is true, sometimes the arguments that are presented do not tend to prove the point. The information that is being offered is therefore not relevant.

As for credibility, you usually know when you do not believe what someone is saying. Sometimes your disbelief is derived from a person's demeanor, from the way they speak or act - the tone of voice, hesitancy in speaking, and lack of eye contact.

You may question information because it comes from an indirect source. When you hear information from a person who does not have personal knowledge of the facts, but only heard the information from someone else, you tend to question it. This type of information is known as hearsay. Hearsay may actually be true, but because it is presented to you by someone without actual knowledge, you may question its accuracy and reliability.

Later in this book we will discuss specific concepts of the rules of evidence and how to rule on objections to evidence. An arbitrator is not bound to enforce the strict legal rules of evidence as a judge is required to do. However, the basic principles behind the evidentiary rules that we apply every day are used in arbitration as aids to the arbitrator in making a reasoned decision, and certainly should not be considered obstacles for the arbitrator who is not an attorney.

8. What information must I ask about the case initially?

Arbitrators are required to disclose past contacts with parties, attorneys, and other individuals who will participate in the arbitration. This disclosure requirement allows the parties to assure themselves that there are no conflicts of interest with regard to the arbitrator's personal and professional contacts that would create bias on the part of the arbitrator.

When you are first appointed as an arbitrator, there are a number of questions you must first ask in order to fulfill your initial duty of disclosure. These questions include:

Who are the parties to the dispute?

Who are the affiliates or subsidiaries of the parties?

What is the subject matter of the dispute? (E.g., the name of the construction project, the product to be delivered.)

Who are the major subcontractors or other interested parties involved in the dispute?

Who are the attorneys for the parties?

Who are the expert witnesses or consultants that are known at the time the arbitration demand is made?

You need to know this information in order to decide if there is any reason why you should not accept the appointment as the arbitrator, because of past contact with any of the participants.

9. What information must I disclose about myself?

You are qualified as an arbitrator because of your experience in a particular industry. It is not uncommon for you to have had contact with many individuals in your industry. Regardless of whether you are arbitrating under the rules of an administering organization or under procedures which you establish with the parties, your initial duty as an arbitrator is to disclose any previous contacts with the participants in the arbitration, whether these contacts were social, professional, regular, or intermittent.

Just as an attorney cannot represent a party against a former client or against someone with whom the attorney has a personal relationship, an arbitrator may not be able to render an impartial decision if he or she has had prior contacts with a party, witness, or anyone else involved in the arbitration. I say *may not* be able to, because your having had prior contact with one or more of the individuals with an interest or role in the arbitration does not necessarily mean that your impartiality as an arbitrator will be affected.

Only after you receive full information as to the background and the participants will you be able to make full disclosure as to previous contacts with the participants. The parties may not be able to supply all of the information immediately, especially the names of expert witnesses and consultants if none have been retained. It is important that you ask the questions as soon as possible. Failure to disclose past contacts, no matter how insignificant they may seem, is a subject that may take on greater significance the longer the disclosure is withheld. Past contact and disclosure do not mean that you will be disqualified, or that you should disqualify yourself, as the arbitrator. If you and the parties are convinced that the past contact will not affect your impartiality, you should not be disqualified.

I was once involved in a situation in which an attorney representing one of the parties and the arbitrator were both members of the same section of the American Bar Association. They saw each other once or twice a year at bar functions. They were on a first-name basis as a result of this professional contact. Neither the attorney nor the arbitrator disclosed the prior contact when the arbitrator was appointed by the administering organization.

The day before the hearing, the arbitrator held a conference call to discuss procedural issues. During the conference call, the attorney who had previously had contact with the arbitrator called him by his first name. The other attorney immediately asked how the arbitrator and the attorney were on a first-name basis. They revealed their past professional contact. The other attorney asked the arbitrator to withdraw.

The case was a complicated commercial contract with substantial claims and counterclaims. Ten days of hearing were scheduled. The arbitrator felt that his prior contact with one of the attorneys would not affect his impartiality. The other attorney's challenge and request to withdraw the day before the hearing, however, caused the arbitrator to be reluctant to invest ten days conducting a hearing, knowing that the other party might claim bias if it did not prevail in the arbitration. The arbitrator withdrew, a new arbitrator had to be appointed, and the hearing was substantially delayed. The failure to immediately disclose allowed a party to question the impartiality of the arbitrator and caused the withdrawal of the arbitrator. Had the disclosure been made at the beginning of the proceedings, there would probably have been no objection and the arbitration would have proceeded without the need for the arbitrator to ultimately withdraw.

Even prompt disclosure of innocent and seemingly remote prior contact may result in a request that the arbitrator withdraw. I was once selected as an arbitrator in a construction dispute arising from a condominium project. I was teaching a course in construction law at a local law school, and I remembered that a student several years ago had mentioned that he was employed on the project during the summer. I reviewed my files and identified the student by name. As it turned out, the student's grandfather had an ownership interest in the project. The other party did not want a former professor of one of the owner's relatives as an arbitrator and requested that I not accept the appointment as arbitrator.

The arbitrator may not be able to make a full disclosure at the time of appointment because identities of some participants are not known. It is possible that an arbitrator may recognize an individual witness at a hearing, or a witness may recognize an arbitrator, as someone with whom they have had prior contact. If this occurs, the arbitrator should immediately inform the parties as to the details of the prior contact. Usually, the parties are reluctant to remove an arbitrator who has already begun the hearing, as long as the contact does not affect the arbitrator's impartiality.

In summary, disclose any prior contact as early as possible. Innocent contact disclosed early is often dismissed by the parties. The longer you wait to make a disclosure, the more likely it is that a party may question your impartiality.

10. What documents should I review after I am appointed?

You will want to review the document that the claimant uses to initiate the arbitration, which is called the **arbitration demand**. This may be a simple document that alleges breach of contract and requests a specific dollar amount in damages, or it may be similar to a complaint filed in a lawsuit, containing a detailed description of the dispute and an itemization of damages. The respondent may file a responding document called an **answer** which will deny the claimant's claim. This is usually a very brief document lacking in detail.

You should also review the contract between the parties, and especially the **arbitration clause**. The arbitration clause may designate specific rules of procedure from an administering organization that will govern the proceedings, or may direct the arbitrator and the parties to devise procedures for the arbitration. The arbitration clause may contain other agreements of the parties, such as the number of arbitrators, the location of the hearing, the format of the arbitrator's award, and other matters.

11. Are counterclaims filed in arbitration?

Yes. If the respondent believes it has a claim arising out of the same dispute, it may file a **counterclaim** against the claimant. If a counterclaim is filed, the arbitrator usually decides both the claim and the counterclaim in the same arbitration proceeding. It is possible that both parties have valid claims, and the arbitrator may grant both the claim and the counterclaim. The party whose award exceeds that of the other party is then entitled to the excess of its award over the award to the other party.

Prehearing Procedures and the Preliminary Conference

PREHEARING PROCEDURES AND
THE PRELIMINARY CONFERENCE

12. How do I communicate with the parties after I am appointed?

After your appointment as an arbitrator, it is absolutely essential that your contact with any party be in the presence of all parties. When an arbitrator has contact with only one party, it is called *ex parte* contact. *Ex parte* contact is to be avoided. The most innocent *ex parte* contact with a party to the dispute can be used to discredit your impartiality, and may serve as a ground to **vacate** your award.

Avoiding ex parte contact is easy if you have a staff person who is able to screen your phone calls. Provide the staff person with the names of all participants in the arbitration and give instructions not to put any telephone calls through to you. In the event that calls are received from the participants, the staff person should direct the caller to contact the case administrator at the administering organization. If you are serving as an arbitrator directly appointed by the parties, your staff person should act as the case administrator, and ask the caller the reason for the call. After ascertaining the reason for the call, your staff person should suggest that a conference call be held to resolve the matter, if it requires resolution.

The parties or their attorneys may find the need to call to inquire about scheduling or other procedural matters. You should have your staff person answer these inquiries if possible or arrange a conference call with all attorneys. Do not risk the appearance of partiality by speaking directly to a party or attorney, even to answer such routine inquiries.

If you have no staff person to field these inquires, and you are not working with an administering organization, caution the attorneys that if they have the need for an immediate inquiry they should have the other attorney on a conference line when they call.

13. What do I do after I have been appointed and make the necessary disclosures?

Regardless of the size of the amount in dispute, you should schedule a preliminary conference with the parties and their lawyers. Some call it a preliminary hearing. I prefer to characterize it as a **preliminary conference**.

14. Why do I need a preliminary conference?

There are several reasons for holding a preliminary conference. Since an arbitration demand is not usually a very detailed document, often only a limited amount of information is exchanged in the early stages of arbitration. The parties and their attorneys may have had little or no contact with each other since the dispute arose, except to choose the arbitrator. The preliminary conference gives the parties and their attorneys an opportunity to meet the arbitrator early in the process. A good arbitrator will use the preliminary conference as a forum to discuss and clarify the issues of the dispute.

You should suggest that the attorneys have their clients present, as you want the parties to participate. The preliminary conference is the first opportunity for the parties to face the reality of the arbitration process. The media has created in the public mind a false expectation of the efficiency and drama of the legal process. Television and movies dramatize litigation and present a distorted indication of the time frame involved.

In reality, a commercial dispute is hardly entertaining. The swift and glib questioning of witnesses and the legal gymnastics portrayed in the media are not the norm. Rather, discussion concerning documentation and the import of everyday business actions is often boring and ponderous. At the preliminary conference, the parties may realize for the first time that they are at the beginning of a process that will require their own time as well their attorneys' time and fees. A discussion of the issues in the dispute soon makes it apparent that much effort will be needed to prepare the case and to present it effectively at a hearing. The preliminary conference also provides an opportunity for settlement discussions to take place and for the matter to be resolved. We will cover this topic when we discuss procedures for conducting the preliminary conference.

There is a belief that one does not have the same right of "prehearing discovery" that one would have in litigation. When I first began to serve as an arbitrator, I did not hold preliminary conferences. I set the hearing date by telephone and did not meet the parties until the hearing. The parties would request by subpoena various documents to be produced at the hearing. When the documents were brought to the hearing, the parties asked for the opportunity to inspect the documents before the hearing proceeded. This procedure for document review was employed because there was no previous agreement to exchange information before the hearing. I would either recess the hearing to allow the parties to review the documents, or the parties would proceed in an extremely unprepared manner. This is very inefficient and certainly not conducive to an orderly presentation of evidence at the hearing.

To avoid this inefficiency, you should have the parties during the preliminary conference agree to exchange sufficient information before the hearing begins so that they can prepare for the hearing. This is similar to a discovery schedule that a court establishes in litigation.

15. How do I initiate the preliminary conference?

If the arbitration is administrated by an administering organization, you may have the case administrator contact the attorneys and schedule the preliminary conference. Write a letter to the case administrator, stating that you are requesting a preliminary conference to discuss the issues and schedule further proceedings. Include a list of agenda items. Invite the attorneys and representatives from the parties to attend. **[See Form 1 - Request for Preliminary Conference].** Request that the case administrator forward your letter to the attorneys and set forth your available dates for the preliminary conference.

If there is no administering organization, address the letter to the attorneys jointly and send copies to the attorneys directly.

16. Where is the preliminary conference held?

You will need an office or a conference room, depending on the number attending. I prefer a conference room with a large table. Participants at arbitration proceedings tend to take notes during the proceeding and should be able to do so comfortably, without trying to balance a pad or notebook on their laps.

If you have the physical facilities available, it is preferable to conduct the conference, as well as the hearing, at your own place of business. There are practical reasons for this. A party or its attorney may suggest that they have the necessary facilities available. Unless the other party readily agrees, you should not have the conference at such a non-neutral location. Later, a disgruntled party may attempt to show that you were biased because the conference was held in the offices of one of the parties or its attorney. Your place of business is a logical place to hold the conference. No one should object, unless it is geographically inconvenient. Another alternative is to hold the preliminary conference in the office of the administering organization.

17. How do I conduct the preliminary conference?

The preliminary conference should be informal. If you are having the conference at your place of business, it is best that the participants wait for you in the conference room. When you are informed that all have arrived, enter the conference room and introduce yourself. This assures that you have not had *ex parte* contact before the conference. As the participants introduce themselves, emphasize the informality of the situation by responding, "Mr./Ms. X, a pleasure to meet you." **Even though this is an informal proceeding, resist any temptation to call participants by their first names.**

When everyone is seated, pass around a sign-in sheet for everyone to indicate their name, title, and position. Often, more than one attorney will represent a party or a party may bring more than one representative. The sign-in sheet will help you identify the participants. It is essential that you be aware of the identity and position of everyone attending the preliminary conference.

You should begin the conference by briefly reiterating the agenda that was set forth in your letter requesting a preliminary conference. Explain that while you have read the arbitration demand and any pleadings filed to date, the first matter to be discussed will be a short explanation of the case by both parties. Emphasize that the parties' explanations need not be a detailed discussion of every issue, but are for the purpose of educating you about the major issues of the case.

You should also explain that the preliminary conference is an informal meeting and the parties should feel free to explain their positions. They should not leave this task exclusively to their attorneys. While this suggestion may not sit well with counsel, parties often leap at the chance to tell their story.

18. Why should the parties explain the case to the arbitrator at the preliminary conference?

If you are ultimately going to have a hearing in the case, why have the parties explain the case at the preliminary conference? Allowing the parties to explain the case educates the arbitrator, and allows the parties to begin venting pent up emotions and frustration.

Ask the claimant for an explanation of the case, and then respondent. If the parties themselves, and not their attorneys, seize the opportunity to speak, you often will see emotion and frustration burst forth. This is the first opportunity for the parties to talk to the person who has the authority to decide the case. Often it is the first time that the parties to the dispute have seen each other face to face since the dispute arose. The explanation of the case in the preliminary conference is an important part of the "venting process." After the parties have had their say, you can almost feel tangible relief in the room.

You should make it clear that the preliminary conference is not part of the actual arbitration hearing. Rather, the preliminary conference is held to familiarize the arbitrator, the attorneys and the parties with the issues of the dispute and to schedule the proceedings. Each party will have ample opportunity to present testimony and other evidence at the hearing. Even if a significant discussion about the case occurs during the preliminary conference, the parties cannot refer or rely on that discussion during the subsequent hearing. Any information which the parties wish the arbitrators to consider in reaching a decision must be presented during the arbitration hearing.

The parties may decide to engage in settlement negotiations after the preliminary conference. The realization that the arbitration process has now begun often serves as a reality check to those who feel they would be better served by resolving the matter short of a hearing and a determination by the arbitrator.

19. How do I supervise prehearing discovery?

Inquire if the parties intend to conduct **prehearing discovery**, i.e., review relevant documents in the possession of the parties, respond to written questions (interrogatories), and oral depositions. Such discovery procedures are common in litigation, but are not necessarily a matter of right in arbitration. In most arbitrations, the arbitrator does not have authority to order discovery, unless the parties have agreed in advance to allow discovery to take place. Many parties agree to arbitrate because they know there are no rights to discovery.

Suggest to the parties that the presentation of their cases at the hearing will be accomplished in a more orderly and efficient manner if they agree to a prehearing discovery schedule similar to that used in court. This is preferable to reviewing documentary discovery at the hearing by the use of a subpoena. (See previous discussion concerning subpoenas for documents to be brought to the hearing, in response to Question 14).

One or both parties may object to prehearing discovery because their clients have selected arbitration relying upon the fact that there is not a specific right to discovery. Emphasize that the parties can control the costs of arbitration by agreeing to exchange all information relevant to the dispute before the hearing so that they can have adequate time to prepare their case before the hearing.

It is a rare moment when the parties do not take the arbitrator's suggestion for prehearing discovery. If both parties are represented by attorneys, the attorneys will usually agree to have a structured discovery schedule. Discovery allows them to do their job as they know how to do it. In the long run, a discovery schedule saves the client money, because it increases the efficiency of the process.

20. How do I determine a discovery schedule and a hearing date?

If the parties agree to conduct discovery, schedule the hearing date **before** you discuss the discovery schedule. By setting a hearing date first, you have determined the time period during which discovery can occur. For example, if the hearing date is set six months from the preliminary conference, the parties only have that six month period to conduct discovery.

Once the hearing date has been established, time periods are set for the various methods of discovery that the parties intend to conduct. These include reviewing documents, answering written interrogatories, and taking oral depositions of various witnesses. The documents are usually reviewed and the interrogatories answered before depositions are conducted.

One way to establish the discovery schedule is to give the parties two weeks or some other short period of time after the preliminary conference to agree to a discovery schedule and submit it to you in writing. A better way is to have the parties agree to the specific dates for discovery at the preliminary conference, and then issue an order setting forth the parties agreement as to these dates. **[See Form 2 - Prehearing Order]**

21. What other matters can be discussed at a preliminary conference?

If a claim has many items, I require the claimant to file an itemization of all elements of its claim. This itemization isolates the relative cost of each of the claim elements. There is no reason to spend hours of testimony on a claim item that has minimal value in relation to the entire claim.

If the respondent has not filed a counterclaim, inquire if it intends to do so. Some may think that you are inviting the widening of the dispute, but there is a valid reason for asking. A common tactic is for the respondent to file a counterclaim close to the hearing date in order to delay the hearing. Set a date for filing a counterclaim, and have the parties agree that any counterclaim filed after that date will be the subject of another arbitration.

You may also set a date for exchange of expert reports. This alleviates any last minute surprise with regard to expert opinions to be offered at the hearing. Also discuss whether the parties wish to have a court reporter present during the hearing, and whether they will file posthearing briefs or have closing arguments at the conclusion of the hearing. These topics are discussed in this book in the section addressing the conduct of the hearing.

22. Should I inquire as to the status of settlement discussions?

You may inquire as to the status of settlement discussions during the preliminary conference - but very carefully. You should never mention settlement in such a way as to indicate that you have already made a decision as to the merits of the case. It is appropriate to inquire if there have been any attempts to settle, and if it is possible that the parties may wish to try further.

The positions of the parties may be so conflicting that they have no interest in attempting to settle. Often, however, there is a willingness by both parties to attempt to settle the matter, especially after just having discussed a discovery schedule and setting a hearing date. If the parties have any interest in conducting settlement discussions, the preliminary conference presents an opportunity to do so, since the parties and their attorneys are present. Offer to let the parties have the use of the conference room as long as they like, and leave the room.

The parties may reach a settlement during discussions when they meet for the preliminary conference. Perhaps the dose of reality of the preliminary conference was all they needed to set them on the road to settlement.

23. Should I participate in settlement discussions?

Absolutely not.

24. Why not?

During settlement discussions, parties may discuss matters that are not admissable in court or in arbitration, such as offers of compromise. Offers of compromise are not admissable, because parties would not be able to talk freely and reach a settlement if they knew that their offers to compromise their claims could be used by the other party against them before a judge, jury, or arbitrator. Settlement discussions are therefore not admissible into evidence in court or in arbitration.

If a judge, jury, or an arbitrator were to hear offers of compromise that indicate the extent that parties were willing to forego their claims in order to settle, a false impression might be given of the parties' assessment of the actual merits of their claims.

If you are to make a reasoned decision based on the evidence presented, you should not become involved in settlement discussions. Such participation increases the risk that you may have ex parte contact with one of the parties. If the settlement discussions fail, you have put your own participation in the arbitration process at risk.

25. What if the parties ask me to mediate the dispute?

The parties may request the arbitrator to act as a mediator at any time. This request may occur during or shortly after the preliminary conference, after discovery is concluded, or during the hearing. The request is made when the parties are seriously considering settlement, after they have become acquainted with you and believe that you may be helpful in the settlement process.

We discussed previously the parties' request that the arbitrator "participate" in settlement discussions. This suggests that the arbitrator act as an observer, or offer an opinion as to the viability of settlement options. A request to act as a "mediator" suggests a more participatory involvement in the settlement process. A mediator's role is to facilitate settlement discussions, find common grounds of agreement, meet with the parties separately to discuss confidential information, and otherwise foster a settlement.

Acting as a mediator presents the same issues as participating in settlement discussions. By acting in such a role, you compromise your position as an arbitrator. This occurs because in the role of mediator you may become aware of information you normally would not hear as an arbitrator, such as inadmissable offers of compromise.

There are several caveats for an arbitrator who contemplates mediating a dispute. If you have never been trained as a mediator, do not assume you know how to mediate. Mediation is a completely different dispute resolution technique. There are specific procedures and techniques unique to the mediation process that you should know in order to act successfully as a mediator. Most mediators receive training and then perform their first mediation with the guidance of an experienced mediator.

Even though I am an experienced mediator, my first reaction as an arbitrator when requested to act as a mediator is one of reluctance. I suggest that the parties retain another person to act as a mediator, so that my role as an arbitrator will not be compromised. If I were to act as a mediator, and the parties were unable to reach a settlement, then I would need to withdraw as the arbitrator, because of the type of information I would most likely hear in the mediation process and the *ex parte* contact which I might have with the parties. If the parties insist that I mediate the dispute, I do so only with the agreement that I will no longer be the arbitrator if the mediation fails.

If the request to mediate comes after the hearing begins, I refuse the request to become a mediator, and suggest that another individual be retained as mediator. Otherwise, the parties would have to begin the hearing again with a new arbitrator if I assumed the role of the mediator and the mediation failed.

26. Must I conduct the preliminary conference in person?

For cases of small dollar value, the parties may resist attending a preliminary conference in person. The travel time for the attorneys and the parties to get to the preliminary conference may be worth an excessive amount of legal fees and lost time to the parties compared to the value of the claim. You can still conduct the preliminary conference by telephone, and request that the attorneys and the parties participate.

27. How do I assure the parties abide by the prehearing schedule?

Memorialize the schedule in a prehearing order, setting forth the dates to which the parties have agreed. **[See Form 2 - Prehearing Order]** Also, you can emphasize to the parties that they should promptly bring to your attention any discovery dispute. You can then resolve the discovery dispute, so that there is no delay in the schedule.

28. How do I deal with parties who represent themselves without an attorney?

You should make sure that the parties to the arbitration realize that they have the opportunity to retain legal counsel to represent them. Most parties who represent themselves without the benefit of counsel are at a distinct disadvantage if the opposing party is represented by counsel. As an arbitrator, you are not required to come to the rescue of a person who has chosen to forego legal representation.

Your main concern should be that the unrepresented party understand the "burden of proof," i.e. that which must be proved in order to successfully establish a claim or defend against a claim. Anger and indignation are the ingredients of movies and TV shows, but facts and documentation are essential in order to prevail in litigation and arbitration.

During the preliminary conference, you may discuss the issues and the types of information that the parties will need to present in order for you to arrive at a decision. Hopefully, the parties understand this guidance.

Prehearing
Submissions,
Subpoenas, and
Discovery
Disputes

PREHEARING SUBMISSIONS, SUBPOENAS, AND DISCOVERY DISPUTES

29. What information should the parties exchange before the hearing?

The parties will not necessarily use all the documents produced in discovery as hearing exhibits. The hearing will progress more efficiently if the parties identify and exchange the documents they intend to use as hearing exhibits. Exchange of exhibits should be accomplished at least several days before the hearing begins. This allows the parties to review the documentation to which witnesses will refer when testifying. It is good practice for the arbitrator to become familiar with the documents before the hearing.

You should direct the parties to organize the presentation of the hearing exhibits. You should not have to deal with random pieces of paper during the hearing. To make handling the exhibits easy for all concerned, ask the parties to put their exhibits in a three-ring binder, arranged in chronological order and marked with tabs.

This "Exhibit Book" should contain an index, listing the document by type (e.g., memo, letter), author, individual to whom the document is written, date and exhibit number. The Exhibit Books should be exchanged between the parties and a copy sent to the arbitrator. It is a good idea for each party to bring multiple copies of their Exhibit Books to the hearing, so that the witness can have his or her own copy to review while testifying. I usually will review each party's exhibits shortly before the hearing to familiarize myself with the information that the parties are going to rely upon to prove their cases. If I have questions concerning the exhibits that I might ask a witness, I am careful not to write my comments directly on the exhibits. It is good practice to use removable "post-it" notes.

The parties may submit some of the same documents as exhibits. This is unavoidable, and should not present a problem. Also, there may be exhibits that the parties fail to include in the initial exchange of exhibits. You should not exclude additional exhibits during the hearing if they are offered. We will discuss how to resolve objections to these exhibits if a party objects to their admission on the basis of surprise.

The parties should also submit a witness list, identifying all witnesses they expect to testify at the hearing, and a brief description of the testimony to be offered by each witness. Expert witnesses should be identified as such. The witness list need not include "rebuttal witnesses." Rebuttal witnesses are those witnesses that a party calls to contradict testimony that another witness offers during the hearing. The identities of rebuttal witnesses are not known until testimony is offered that a party makes a determination to rebut by further testimony.

Sometimes the parties wish to submit prehearing briefs. You may tell the parties that prehearing briefs are optional, as they can state a summary of their case in an opening statement at the beginning of the hearing. If the parties insist, do not discourage prehearing briefs.

30. How do I issue subpoenas?

A subpoena is an order by a court, arbitration panel, or other tribunal that requires a person to appear and offer testimony or bring documents relevant to the dispute. In litigation, the party requesting the subpoena fills out a preprinted form or prepares its own form, indicating the identity of the individual or the documents requested. Various organizations that administer arbitration have prepared their own subpoena forms. You can create one for yourself if you have been retained directly by the parties, or request the attorneys to prepare subpoenas for you to review and sign. **[See Form 3 - Subpoena]**

When presented with a subpoena from a party, you must review the nature of the description of the documents requested in order to assure yourself that the documents are relevant. After you sign the subpoena, it is the responsibility of the party to serve the subpoena on the person whose testimony or documents are sought. You have no further responsibility.

Not all witnesses require a subpoena. The standard practice is for the parties to make available all persons and documents within their control. A subpoena is necessary to require persons to appear who are not employed by the parties, or to produce documents which the parties do not possess. Witnesses may request a subpoena, not because they are reluctant to testify, but to justify absence from work.

31. What types of discovery disputes might I be required to resolve?

One party may ask to inspect documents that the other party claims are not relevant or privileged. A party may complain because the other party refuses to answer or does not give a complete answer to a written interrogatory. During a deposition, the person being deposed may refuse to answer a question. If any of these disputes arise, the aggrieved party will usually look to the arbitrator to resolve the matter.

32. How do I resolve discovery disputes?

The key concept that is usually involved in a discovery dispute is relevancy. Relevant information is that which tends to prove or disprove a fact which is necessary to resolve the dispute. If evidence is relevant, the arbitrator should order it disclosed, unless it is privileged.

Most information that you might think is privileged is not. Information that is confidential in the ordinary course of business is not privileged from disclosure in arbitration if it is relevant to the dispute. Unless the information is attorney-client, doctor-patient, or husband-wife communication, you should request a written explanation as to why a party believes certain information is privileged from disclosure.

If a party refuses to produce a document that the arbitrator believes is relevant, the arbitrator can ultimately draw a *negative inference* in reaching his or her decision. This means that the arbitrator can assume that the document would have supported the position of the party who requested the production of the document.

33. What if a person who has received a subpoena fails to appear at the hearing?

Unfortunately, you cannot enforce the subpoena. The party who served the subpoena may file a suit in court to enforce the subpoena if the law of the state where the arbitration is held permits this procedure.

34. What happens if the hearing concludes before a party enforces a subpoena?

After the hearing is concluded, you can "continue" the hearing for a specific time period, i.e., keep the record open, and allow the testimony or documents to be presented at a future date, if a court enforces the subpoena. You should not leave the record open indefinitely. After a specified period, if the court does not enforce the subpoena, the record should be closed, and the award should be rendered based upon the evidence which has been received.

Conducting the Hearing

CONDUCTING THE HEARING

35. How may a party attempt to delay the hearing?

Shortly before the hearing, a party may attempt to delay the hearing. There are, of course, legitimate, unexpected reasons for delaying a hearing - illness, death, or mutual agreement to enter into settlement discussions. On the other hand, a party or an attorney may attempt to delay for personal reasons - lack of preparation, difficulties with legal representation, demands of business, or other reasons particular to the party. In legal terminology, a request to postpone a hearing before the hearing begins, or to suspend a hearing after it has begun, is known as a **continuance.**

36. How do I deal with attempts to delay the hearing?

The best prevention of unnecessary delays to the hearing is to issue a stern warning to the parties during the preliminary conference that delays in *any* of the dates established in the schedule will be granted only for "good cause." What is good cause? That is for you to determine, based upon the facts of the situation.

If a party requests a delay in the commencement of the hearing, and the other party objects, you must determine if there is good cause to reschedule the hearing. Schedule a conference call to resolve the issue. Time is of the essence in resolving the request for continuance, so *do not* have the parties submit their positions in writing. If you do, it will be difficult to assess the credibility of the party requesting the continuance, and only delay the resolution of the issue.

During the conference call, explore the reasons for the delay. If an attorney requests the delay because of a sudden crisis in the office, suggest that another attorney handle the matter. After all, there has been adequate notice of the hearing, and everyone has made efforts to make themselves available. If illness is alleged, ask about the details of the illness. Miraculous healings may occur as you press for details. If the request is based upon the unavailability of a witness, you can suggest that the hearing proceed and the witness can testify out of order, or at the end of the hearing. If unavailability of a party representative is the reason for the request, explore the availability of another party representative.

Be your own advocate against a delay that you feel is unjustified. You have cleared your own schedule for the hearing, and you may not be able to conveniently reschedule the hearing in the near future. Carefully explore any objections made by the parties to a request to delay the hearing. I once had an attorney tell me that the hearing could not be delayed because the matter previously had been filed in court and the judge had then ordered that it be submitted into arbitration to be concluded by a certain date.

The arbitration had been pending for several months, and that was the first time I had been made aware of a court order concerning the case. I asked for a copy of the court order, and *never* received it, despite my repeated requests. The requesting party demonstrated good cause to postpone the hearing, and it was postponed. When the hearing commenced, the lawyer who made the misrepresentation as to the existence of the court order had been replaced by another attorney in his office.

37. What facilities do I need for the hearing?

You will need a conference room with a large conference table. You will also need an area outside the hearing room for witnesses to wait, and for attorneys and the parties to confer. If you have the facilities, it is best to conduct the hearing at your place of business.

38. What seating arrangement do I use for the hearing?

A long, rectangular table is preferable. The arbitrator should sit on the end with the parties on either side. The witness who is testifying should sit next to the arbitrator, and the position opposite the witness should be left vacant, so that the arbitrator can use it for reviewing exhibits and other documents. This allows the arbitrator sufficient room to take notes and also keeps the other participants at a distance so they cannot see the arbitrator's notes. The witness will want the "friendly attorney", (i.e., the one representing the party for whom the witness is testifying), to sit next to him. Party representatives sit next to their respective attorneys. The arrangement is as follows:

Witness Attorney Party

Arbitrator   [TABLE]

[Empty] Attorney Party

If a court reporter is present, the reporter should sit in the empty position opposite the witness. The reporter types on a stenography machine that does not require table space, and this leaves room for the arbitrator's documents.

In disputes where parties appear without lawyers, a different seating arrangement may be used. The arbitrator may sit on one side of the table facing both parties, and have the parties sit next to each other:

Arbitrator

[TABLE]

Party #1   Party #2

This arrangement keeps both parties facing the arbitrator, rather than facing each other. In this arrangement, you do not have to turn your head from side to side to effectively view evidence and the parties.

39. What is the general procedure for the hearing?

An arbitration hearing is similar to a trial in court, but less formal. The hearing begins by having the parties (or their lawyers) give brief opening statements. If the parties have filed prehearing briefs, a party may dispense with an opening statement.

The claimant then calls its witnesses, and asks questions of each witness by direct examination. The respondent is allowed to cross-examine the witness, and the claimant can then conduct redirect examination on issues raised in cross-examination. The respondent may then recross-examine the witness on issues raised on redirect examination, if necessary. The arbitrator may also ask the witness questions. When the parties and the arbitrator conclude their questioning, the witness is excused.

After the claimant presents its witnesses, the respondent calls its witnesses. The respondent may have a counterclaim, and it will then present testimony to support the counterclaim. If the respondent does not have a counterclaim, the testimony will be offered to rebut and defend against claimant's claim.

After the parties present their witness, they each have an opportunity to call "rebuttal witnesses." Rebuttal witnesses are called in order to rebut testimony that was presented at the hearing. Rebuttal witnesses may be witnesses that have already testified, or they may be new witnesses, depending on the subject matter being rebutted.

After the testimony is concluded, the parties' attorneys may present closing arguments. Closing arguments summarize what each party believes it has proved in the hearing, and what each believes the other has failed to prove. In lieu of, or in addition to, closing arguments, the parties may file posthearing briefs, usually within thirty days of the hearing, unless the parties request a longer period of time for a complex case. After closing arguments or receipt of posthearing briefs, the record is closed and the case is ready for an award to be rendered.

40. How do I perform my duties during the hearing?

Like everything else in life, being an arbitrator has two requirements. You have to *do what you have to do* and you have to *look like you know what you are doing.* Remember, the parties have conferred authority upon you. While you are doing what you have to do, you need to convince the parties that you are doing it correctly.

So, what is it that you have to do? First and foremost, you have to **listen and understand** the arguments and testimony. Not only must you listen and understand, but you should also **clarify** whatever is not clear to you. Ask questions and require witnesses to explain their testimony until you are sure you understand the parties' positions. If a witness is talking too fast, politely ask the witness to slow down. Take notes if necessary.

How do you look like you know what you are doing? Use body language. Sit erect, keep your eyes open, and look at the witness who is testifying. Request that the witnesses and attorneys address their remarks to you. Fight the tendency to lean forward in your chair. Do not lean forward with your chin in your hand. Lean back, with your spine against the back of the chair. You will be presiding over parties who are in the midst of emotional and economic turmoil. Develop a calm "**judicial temperament**."

41. What is the difference between argument and testimony?

Opening statements and closing arguments are usually made by attorneys. Keep in mind that attorneys are not witnesses - they were not involved in the events that have given rise to the dispute, and they have no personal knowledge of the facts and circumstances. They are therefore framing the facts in argumentative terms, in order to present the facts in a light most favorable to their clients. There is nothing wrong with this - that is what they are trained to do, and that is what clients pay them to do.

Learn to distinguish argument from fact. Interpretation of facts presented in arguments may not be supported by the testimony or by the documents submitted as hearing exhibits. Look to the testimony and the exhibits to make certain that they support the parties' positions.

An opening statement by an attorney may describe testimony that will be offered at the hearing. Listen carefully to the testimony. The witness may or may not testify exactly as the "preview" in the opening statement has described.

42. What can I do if an opening statement is too long?

In one of my earliest cases as an arbitrator, an attorney gave a two-hour opening statement. During the hearing, I realized that the lengthy opening statement had been offered so that the attorney could stall for time, because he had failed to adequately prepare his case. Lengthy opening statements are not offered often, but when this occurs you should deal with it diplomatically. I had another occasion when I believed the opening statement was getting out of hand, and I requested that the attorney "summarize, if possible" the remainder of his opening statement in the interest of time. He took the hint, and concluded quickly.

43. Who is allowed in the hearing room?

Court proceedings are usually open to the public - arbitration is not. Parties often choose arbitration because it is private. The parties and their attorneys are allowed in the hearing room. Other necessary persons, such as those who will serve as expert witnesses or consultants aiding in the presentation or preparation of a party's case, may also be allowed in the hearing room.

There is no public record of an arbitration. It is a private matter, conducted by an agreement of the parties. Arbitrations are usually held in non-public environments - private offices, hotel conference rooms, or other venues where the general public does not have ready access. Even if the public is aware that the arbitration is taking place, there is no public "right to know." Any inquiry from the media should be politely rebuffed by a "no comment" response.

44. What about witnesses who are not parties or necessary persons?

Every person who is to offer testimony as a witness may not be a party or a necessary person. As a general rule, witnesses may not be allowed in the hearing room except to offer testimony. This is known as the "**rule on witnesses**." The reason for the "rule on witnesses" is that a witness should offer testimony without being influenced by the testimony of other witnesses. While a party has the right to be present during the entire hearing (even if that party is also going to be a witness), a witness who is not a party may be excluded from the hearing except to give testimony.

For example, if the case involves a construction dispute between the owner and a contractor, the owner's superintendent may be a witness to various occurrences, but is not a party to the dispute. The superintendent is only there to testify as to the facts within his personal knowledge. Such a witness may be excluded from the hearing room except to give testimony, if the decision is made to invoke the rule on witnesses and exclude witnesses.

Notice that I say *if* the rule on witnesses is invoked. The parties may prefer to have all witnesses present in the hearing room throughout the conduct of the hearing, and the arbitrator may honor this request.

45. What if the parties want the witnesses in the room and I don't?

I always prefer to invoke the rule on witnesses and exclude the witnesses. I believe this procedure provides more credible testimony. I invoke the rule, even if the parties do not. Again, this is personal preference.

I find that if witnesses are not excluded, the testimony that is offered is usually as follows: **"Just as you heard Mr. X say before, what happened was . . ."**

I prefer to hear the facts presented by each of the witnesses, rather than have them validate what others have said and then adopt the testimony as their own.

46. How do I avoid ex parte contact with the parties during the hearing?

The hearing presents an ongoing situation which requires the arbitrator to exercise even more caution and effort to avoid *ex parte* contact. If you conduct the hearing at your place of business, you have an opportunity to reduce the risk of improper contact with the parties. It is good practice to remain in your office during breaks in the hearing, and instruct your staff to physically intercept any of the participants if they appear intent upon having contact with you.

The contact may be as innocent as someone at the hearing wanting to know the location of the copy machine or the restroom. You can avoid these routine questions by introducing a staff member to the participants before the hearing begins. Inform the participants that the staff person is available to answer questions, send or receive faxes, make necessary copies, and perform any other administrative task.

If possible, do not wait in the hearing room for the participants to arrive. Let them arrive and take their seats before you enter. Otherwise, you may find yourself alone in the room with the party, attorney or witness who arrives first.

Be careful what you say in the restroom. You never know who may be in there or walk in while you are there. Your fellow employees may know that a hearing is taking place in the office, and ask you questions if they happen to see you outside the hearing room. Your best response is no response. The arbitration should not be a topic of general discussion at your place of business, as the proceedings are confidential.

Do not accept any rides with any of the participants. If you have the hearing at your office, this is usually not an issue. But if the hearing is held at another location, avoid any offer of transportation. What begins as a offer of courtesy may end up as a challenge to your award by a party who saw you drive away with the other party or its attorney.

47. How do I deal with parties who are not represented by counsel at the hearing?

We have discussed this topic briefly in relation to the preliminary conference. If a party appears without representation, you should confirm at the beginning of the hearing that the party was made aware of the opportunity to retain to legal representation and has chosen not to retain counsel.

Some parties are able to adequately represent themselves, while others are not so capable. A party without legal representation at the hearing may appear to be at a distinct disadvantage. Resist the urge to assist the unrepresented party. You may, however, ask questions of the witnesses for your own information. Remember, your role is not to represent someone who has chosen to forego legal representation, even if that choice was made for financial reasons.

48. Is a court reporter and transcript required?

There is no requirement in arbitration that there be an official record or transcript. Even so, the parties often have a court reporter present. They may order daily transcripts in order to review the witnesses' testimony prior to cross-examination, or a final transcript to assist in their preparation of closing arguments or posthearing briefs. The cost of the transcript is borne by the parties, not the arbitrator or the administering organization.

The parties may agree to have a court reporter present and agree that the transcript is the official record of the proceedings. It is not unusual for one party to want a transcript and the other party not to want it. In that instance, the transcript is not the official record unless the parties thereafter agree that it is, or the arbitrator designates it as such. The arbitrator does not arrange for the court reporter, nor is the arbitrator responsible to pay the court reporter if the parties fail to do so.

49. Do I need a transcript in order to make my decision?

My personal preference is not to have a transcript. I take extensive notes and listen carefully. I ask questions of the witness if I need clarification. The typical arbitration award is not a detailed opinion. It does not contain the arbitrator's reasoning nor reference evidence that the parties have submitted. During my deliberation after the hearing, I do not need, nor want, to relive the hearing by reading the transcript.

On the other hand, I know arbitrators who prefer to have a transcript, because it relieves them of the necessity of taking notes and gives them a second chance to review the testimony. Some arbitrators routinely request the parties to have a court reporter and agree that the transcript is the official record. Whether or not you want a transcript is a personal choice. You may want to request one, just to be safe. As you gain experience, you will decide whether you find a transcript useful.

50. What if the parties ask me if I need a court reporter and a transcript?

Tell them if you prefer to have a transcript. Even though a transcript increases the expense to the parties, request one if you feel you need it. Make it clear that the parties must bear the expense — not the arbitrator or the administering association.

There are various methods of court reporting, and some are better than others. I prefer those who type on a stenography machine. The machine is silent, not distracting, and the transcript is usually highly accurate.

Some reporters merely record the proceedings on a tape recorder and have the recordings transcribed. I find these transcripts may not be as accurate as those produced by the stenography machine. The person who types the transcript from the tapes is not necessarily the one who was present at the hearing.

The method of court reporting that I like least is the "steno mask." This is a compromise between the stenography machine and the tape recorder. A reporter using the steno mask repeats everything that is said into a microphone. In order not to disturb the proceedings, the microphone is in a big plastic mask that looks like an oxygen mask, and absorbs the sound. I find it very distracting to have someone mumbling into the steno mask, and occasionally come up gasping for air.

51. Should I take notes during the hearing?

You may want to do so, even if there is a court reporter and ultimately there will be a transcript. I find that taking notes helps me frame my own questions for the witnesses. I may write down questions that I want to ask the witness while I am listening to testimony. I also review my notes at the end of each day to reinforce what I have heard. Even if there is a transcript, the arbitrator may not receive it until several weeks after the hearing is concluded. Until then, the arbitrator's notes are the only record the arbitrator has during this interim period.

Keep your hearing notes in a notebook or hole punch them and put them in a file. **Never allow the parties or their attorneys to see your notes.** You should always take your notes with you when you leave the hearing room. Do not leave them on the table for anyone to see, or worse yet, for someone to pick up by mistake. See the response to question 92 concerning how you should dispose of your notes after the hearing.

52. May I question the witnesses?

Yes. It is your right to ask questions. If something is unclear, ask the witness to clarify an answer during the testimony. Otherwise, wait until the attorneys question the witness and then ask your substantive questions. The questions you want to ask may ultimately be asked by the attorneys, so it is good practice for the arbitrator to wait and ask questions last. Your questions and the responses of the witness may cause the attorneys to ask additional questions of the witness.

53. If the parties do not ask a question I believe is important, should I ask the question?

Absolutely! If you think it is important, ask the question. Sometimes the question will reveal a weakness in the case of one or both parties. Regardless of the effect of the answer to the question on the presentation of the case, you have the right to ask it and receive an answer.

54. What should I not do during a hearing?

Do not make any notes on your copies of the exhibits. If you find an exhibit of particular interest, put a paper clip on it. Do not make any underlinings or editorial remarks that could come back to haunt you. After you render the award, remove the paper clips or "post-it" notes before returning the exhibits to the administering organization or to the parties.

Do not make any comments about the testimony. Sometimes a witness will make a point of speaking directly to the arbitrator, seeking approval for what they are saying. When you listen to testimony, do not nod your head as if in agreement with anything that is said.

Do not allow yourself to be constantly interrupted to take care of other business during the arbitration. While some interruptions are inevitable, you need to give the arbitration your full attention, and should not look preoccupied with other matters. This caveat also applies to the participants. They should arrange their schedule so that they do not need to be constantly interrupted during the hearing to tend to other matters. *Do not leave your cell phone on and direct all present to turn off their phones.*

55. What if a party wants to postpone the hearing because a witness becomes ill?

You should avoid postponing the hearing unless absolutely necessary. A witness may become ill or otherwise unavailable and a party will attempt to recess the hearing until the witness becomes available. You should offer to hear the testimony of the party's witnesses "out of order," i.e., hear the testimony of the next witness even if the party did not plan to present the witnesses in that order. It does not matter in which order you hear the witnesses. It is more important to keep the hearing moving forward. Remember, it has to be a witness from the same party who is testifying. You should not take a witness for the respondent until the claimant finishes presenting its case. Suggest to the parties that they may take a break for several hours, if there is no witness currently present at the location of the hearing.

56. What if the respondent fails to respond to the arbitration demand?

When an arbitration clause is included in the contract, a party has a right to arbitrate a dispute, even if the other party breaches that agreement by failing to participate. If a party fails to respond to an arbitration demand, you should notify the recalcitrant party that the arbitration is proceeding and continue to give notice as to prehearing deadlines and the hearing date.

Certified return-receipt mail is the most effective and inexpensive way to give notice. The postal service will attempt to obtain a signature several times. Even if the non-responding party does not accept a certified letter, you have a record of your attempt to give notice.

57. Does the claimant automatically prevail if the respondent does not appear at the hearing?

No. A claimant does not prevail by default, i.e., because of the other party's failure to appear and defend itself. The claimant must present its case. The arbitrator must review the evidence and make a decision based upon the evidence. Even if the liability is clear, you should carefully review the support for the damages claimed.

At my first arbitration as an arbitrator, in a relatively small matter, the respondent failed to appear. I called the case administrator at the administering organization and confirmed that the party had received notice of the hearing. I proceeded with the hearing, and had the claimant's attorney present an opening argument and the claimant gave testimony. I reviewed the documentation supporting the damages and asked questions concerning the damage calculation. The claimant prevailed, but I did not award the total amount that was claimed, because the claimant did not support a portion of the damages.

58. Do witnesses testify under oath?

Witnesses testify under oath in arbitration. If there is a court reporter present, the court reporter is usually a notary public and authorized to administer an oath. You may ask the court reporter to administer the oath to the witness. I prefer to do it myself. I use the standard oath you have heard many times on TV or in the movies:

Please state your full name.

Please raise your right hand.

Mr./Ms. Witness, do your solemnly swear or affirm that the testimony you are about to give

in this proceeding will be the truth, the whole truth, and nothing but the truth.

Look the witness in the eye as you administer the oath. This is your first chance to begin assessing credibility and truthfulness. Is the witness looking you in the eye, avoiding your gaze, smirking, smiling, frowning? Is the witness exhibiting arrogance or humility?

59. How is the oath administered to a witness testifying through an interpreter?

A witness may testify in his or her native language through an interpreter. The interpreter administers the oath. You must first place the interpreter under oath. The interpreter is not sworn to tell the truth, as the interpreter's function is to translate the witness's testimony. The interpreter has no ability or responsibility to know whether the witness is telling the truth. Instead, the interpreter is sworn to accurately and faithfully *translate* the questions of the attorneys and the testimony of the witness:

> **Mr./Ms. Interpreter, please raise your right hand. Please state your name. Please state your occupation and qualifications as an interpreter. Do your solemnly swear or affirm that your interpretation of the examination and testimony in this proceeding will be complete and accurate?**

You may then place the witness under oath through the interpreter.

Evidence and Objections

EVIDENCE AND OBJECTIONS

60. Will the attorneys make objections to evidence?

Objections are a common practice in arbitration. It is the responsibility of the arbitrator to rule on objections and either admit or exclude evidence. If you admit evidence, you may rely upon it in reaching your decision; if you exclude evidence, you may not rely upon it. You should direct the attorney making the objection to fully explain the basis of the objection, and request the opposing attorney to state a response to the objection before you make a ruling. The response to the objection may more fully explain the reason why the testimony or documentation is being offered, and will possibly aid you in making your ruling.

61. What are the most common objections?

The most common objections to questions and testimony are those dealing with relevance, leading questions, hearsay, and lack of foundation.

The objections to documents are similar to objections to testimony in some respects. The documents may not be relevant. Many documents are hearsay. The author may not be present, and the objecting party may not have an opportunity to cross-examine the author. Summary documents may not be fully supported by other documentation.

62. How do I resolve the objection that evidence is not relevant?

An objection that information sought is not relevant means that the person making the objection does not believe that the testimony in response to a question or the subject matter of a document is germane to the dispute. The testimony would therefore not tend to prove or disprove a material fact necessary to resolve the dispute.

Before you decide to rule on an objection based on relevancy, you should ask the attorney or party who is examining the witness to state why he or she believes that the information sought by the question is necessary to resolve the dispute.

Even if you think testimony or a document is not relevant, you may decide to admit it. Otherwise, you run the risk of excluding evidence that is relevant and thereby creating a ground for vacating your award. This is truly one of the disadvantages of the arbitration process. Often you err on the side of caution, and endure listening to evidence that you know is not relevant so as not to risk exclusion of relevant evidence.

63. How do I resolve an objection that a question is leading?

A leading question is one which clearly implies its own answer. Excessive use of leading questions results in the witness adopting the lawyer's questions as testimony.

Leading questions are allowed in eliciting information from a witness about which there is no dispute, in order to speed up the testimony. For example, questions concerning personal background are generally leading, but allowable:

And where did you receive your college education?

After graduating from college, where were you first employed?

Both of these questions imply the answer - the witness went to college and thereafter was employed.

Leading questions are not allowed to elicit testimony of essential events. For example:

And when you saw the building fell on Mr. X and crush him beyond recognition, what exactly did you see?

You probably know the classic leading question -**"When did you stop beating your wife?"** The question implies that the witness beat his wife. The question is not only leading, but argumentative, as it implies a fact which is not in evidence and may or may not be true.

64. What is hearsay?

There are lengthy treatises written on hearsay, and a major portion of the study of evidence in law school is devoted to this topic. In reading the following discussion, you should keep in mind that you need not make rulings based on the detailed principles discussed, as **hearsay is generally admissible into evidence in arbitration.** As an arbitrator, you should be familiar with the basic concepts of hearsay.

For our purposes, we need to define hearsay and establish a general principle governing its admission in arbitration.

> *Hearsay* **is a statement or assertive conduct made out of court which is offered in court to prove the truth of the matter asserted.**

Is that clear? Probably not. Generally, it means that hearsay is testimony by someone in court about something that another person said or did out of court which is offered by the witness to prove what the other individual said or did was true.

Hearsay can also be "double hearsay" or "triple hearsay," depending on how many people the information passed through before it was received by the witness. This is testimony such as **"I heard that X told Y that Z said that ..."** Obviously, the credibility of the testimony diminishes with each level.

Let's use an example.

> **Attorney #1: What did the driver say after the accident?**
>
> **Attorney #2: [Before the witness can answer]. Objection. This witness cannot testify as to what the driver said. It would be hearsay.**

At this point, the arbitrator does not know why the testimony is being offered. Suppose the testimony is to prove that the driver was speeding, and the testimony is:

> **Witness: After the accident, I heard the driver of the car say, "I was driving too fast."**

If the statement is offered to prove the truth of the matter asserted, i.e., the driver was driving too fast, it is what is known as an admission against interest, and admissible as evidence. Admissions against interest may or may not be considered hearsay, depending on the rules of evidence to be applied. Under the Federal Rules of Evidence, this testimony is admissible as an admission against the interest of the party making the statement, and therefore not considered hearsay. Other rules of evidence, applied by state courts, may consider an admission against interest hearsay, but allow its admission into evidence as an exception to the hearsay rule.

What if the testimony is offered instead to prove that the driver of the car was conscious after the accident? It would then not be hearsay, as it is not offered to prove the truth of the matter asserted, i.e., that the driver was driving too fast. Rather, it is offered to prove that the driver was able to and did speak, and was therefore conscious.

This shows you the dilemma one faces when dealing with testimony which is potentially hearsay. The content of the testimony is not necessarily sufficient to determine if it is hearsay. One needs to know *why* the testimony is offered into evidence. Once the purpose of the testimony is determined, one then can decide if the testimony is hearsay, not hearsay, or hearsay which is admissible as an exception to the hearsay rule.

65. How do I rule on hearsay objections?

While hearsay may not be admissable in a jury trial, judges who serve in "bench" trials without a jury routinely admit hearsay, and weigh the evidence themselves. Arbitrators act in the same fashion, as they must weigh the evidence themselves.

As difficult as the subject of hearsay may seem, it should not be cause for alarm. As an arbitrator, you are allowed to admit hearsay testimony.

Admission of testimony does not mean that you accept the testimony as true or give it great weight. Exclusion of evidence can serve as a ground to vacate the award, so you should admit hearsay testimony. Only you and your fellow panel members (if you are on a panel) will ever know the weight which you accord to the hearsay testimony.

66. What does objection for "lack of foundation" mean?

This objection is appropriate when the witness begins testifying as to certain matters without first testifying as to the basis of his or her knowledge. For example, if a project manager for a construction project begins testifying as to defective work performed by a contractor, without first informing the arbitrator that he was on site daily and had the personal responsibility for inspecting work performed, one might object to the testimony for "lack of foundation." When this objection is made, you should request that the witness explain the basis of his or her knowledge, before testifying as to the specific events.

67. Must the person who authored a document testify before I can admit a document into evidence?

Usually the author of a document is the person who is called to testify about the document. However, suppose a letter is written by an individual, a vice president of the company, and the letter contains relevant facts. That vice president is still employed by the party offering the letter into evidence, but for some reason he is not available to testify. Another vice president, who did not write the letter, begins to testify as to the content of the letter. The witness may have no personal knowledge of the occurrences described in the letter. At most, the witness may authenticate the document, by identifying the signature of his fellow worker.

If the document is offered into evidence to prove the truth of that which is described in the letter, it is hearsay, as discussed above. While you may admit it, you will have to determine what weight to give to the document in your deliberations. You should also explore the reasons why the author of the letter has not been made available for testimony. The weight you give the document will be determined by whether the reasons for the author's lack of availability seem credible.

Another way a document may be used is to "refresh the recollection" of the witness who is testifying. A document containing a reference to specific information is shown to the witness in order to ascertain if the witness has knowledge of the information or events referenced. A document used to refresh recollection need not be written by the witness, but need only contain information about the subject matter of the dispute.

68. How do I rule on objections to documents?

One of the standard grounds for attempting to vacate an arbitrator's award is to allege that the arbitrator excluded relevant evidence. For this reason, I usually admit most documents. I direct the objecting party to explain the objection, and admit the documents:

> **I note your objection, but the documents are admitted. After hearing the testimony concerning the documents, I will decide the weight I will accord them.**

Admitting relatively few documents into evidence for fear of excluding relevant evidence is acceptable. However, if a party attempts to burden the record with voluminous documents that are clearly not relevant, I tend to scrutinize them carefully before burdening the record with the documents.

69. What other types of evidence may be offered besides testimony and documents?

Parties may offer exhibits that did not exist when the dispute arose but were prepared to be used during the arbitration. For example, a party may offer a model of a building to illustrate the actual project that is the subject of the dispute. If the case involves a car accident, a party may offer a computerized demonstration of the causes of the accident. Such models and demonstrations are representations of the actual events that caused the dispute, but are not objects that existed at the time the dispute arose. They serve to demonstrate those facts that have been offered into evidence by testimony and documentation. This is known as **demonstrative evidence**.

When demonstrative evidence is offered, the parties should establish how the model or demonstration was created, including the information used to create it. Expert testimony is often offered to establish why a model or demonstration is a correct representation of the events. It is a proper objection to demonstrative evidence that it is not a fair representation of the events that it attempts to demonstrate.

70. Are summaries of documents proper evidence?

Summaries of documents may be offered into evidence under appropriate circumstances. The party offering the summary should describe the documentation that is summarized and the method used to compile the summary. Testimony should be offered by the person who prepared the underlying information and by the person who prepared the summary, as the person who prepared the information may not necessarily be the one who prepared the summary.

The summary may be an explanation of events during performance of a contract, an overview of financial information, a collation of weather information, or a collection of data pertinent to the dispute. Summaries may take the form of charts, spreadsheets, chronologies, outlines, computer graphics, or other visual modes of representation.

It is important that you realize that a summary is merely a convenient means of illustrating large amounts of information. The other party cannot challenge the accuracy of summary unless it has been given the opportunity to review the underlying information. If it has not been given the opportunity to do so, you should request that the underlying information be produced and allow the other party the opportunity to review it before proceeding with cross-examination on the summary. This may require that you recess the hearing for a period of time to allow the reviewing party sufficient time to analyze the information.

71. What weight do I give to evidence?

The weight you accord to evidence depends on your own determination of relevance and credibility. Unless you are required to render an award which details your findings of fact and conclusions of law, the parties will never know upon which documents or testimony you have relied to arrive at your decision. Having admitted the documents and testimony, your award cannot be challenged for exclusion of evidence.

72. May I visit the site of the dispute?

If you are an arbitrator for a construction dispute, it is often helpful to visit the site before or during the hearing. You should visit the site of a dispute only with all parties present. Never just go wandering down to the site without the parties present. You risk being accused of **ex parte** contact. You need the parties present so each party can give you its explanation of what you are viewing.

Witness Testimony
and
Closing Arguments

WITNESS TESTIMONY
AND CLOSING ARGUMENTS

73. Should I suggest to the parties how they should prepare their cases for the hearing?

The parties have a burden of proof, and you should neither instruct nor direct a party how to present its case. Such instruction or directions may be interpreted as bias or partiality. If you are having a problem following the presentation of evidence, however, it is proper to suggest to both parties a method of organizing and presenting evidence to aid in your understanding of the evidence.

I was an arbitrator in a case that dealt with the replacement of windows. There were several different types of windows to be replaced on more than thirty buildings. After the first day of the hearing, the presentation of the evidence consisted of testimony and documentation that dealt randomly with the job progress. There was no possible way I could sort out the testimony.

I had a conference with the attorneys and explained that the order of the evidence was chaotic, and simply offering random information to the arbitrator was not going to lend itself to a resolution to the case. The task of the arbitrator is not to receive random information and compile it into an orderly presentation.

We devised a chart on which they could list the buildings, the type of windows, the delivery dates, the installation dates, and all other relevant information. I gave the parties the option of preparing the same chart, and then comparing their two charts to see where they disagreed, or jointly preparing the chart and highlighting their disagreements. The parties welcomed the suggestion.

74. How do I deal with a hostile witness?

Remember that a witness may not be a party to the arbitration, and may not want to testify. Often, witnesses are past employees of the parties who have little loyalty to their former employer. When they are present at the hearing, they are absent from their jobs.

The most effective way to focus a hostile witness is to show empathy, and to suggest that once the testimony is concluded the witness will be excused.

> **Mr./Ms. X, I realize that you are taking time off from work, not necessarily by choice. We appreciate your coming here today. Please listen carefully to the questions that are asked, and confine your answer to the questions. After the attorneys ask their questions, I may have some questions for you also. As soon as your testimony is finished, you can be on your way.**

75. How do I deal with a hostile party?

A hostile party presents a greater problem to the arbitration process than a hostile witness, because, unlike the hostile witness, the hostile party is present throughout the hearing. It is important that party hostility be defused in its early stages, so that you can manage the hearing effectively.

A hostile party is actually breaching the agreement to arbitrate, by abrogating the arbitration process. In admonishing a hostile party, you must emphasize that the parties voluntarily chose to proceed in arbitration. Therefore, the process can only be effective with the cooperation of the parties.

The following example illustrates an arbitrator's diplomacy in dealing with a hostile party:

> **Mr./Ms. X, I realize this dispute has taken its toll on everyone, but I must remind you that it was the parties' choice to arbitrate the dispute. Unless everyone cooperates, the process is not going to be effective. The parties have had ample time to vent their emotions with each other, but now that we are at the hearing stage, I would ask that you control yourself and give your attention to the matters at hand, so that we may proceed.**

76. How do I deal with a hostile attorney?

Attorney hostility is more difficult to define. The task of zealously representing a client lends itself to vigorous actions which may become counterproductive to the orderly presentation of evidence during the hearing. Attorney hostility takes many forms, including bickering with opposing counsel and continuing objections that interrupt testimony.

When continuing objections are made to testimony, the witness may become flustered and not give complete answers. This is often the goal of continuing objections. To put a stop to continuing objections, you should note the objection, and request that the witness be allowed to testify without further objection.

> **Mr./Ms. X, I note your objection and understand the basis for it. However, having overruled your objection I would like to hear the witness testify without further interruption. I will assume that your objection is continuing, so there is no need to reiterate it.**

Attorneys bickering with each other can be stopped by suggesting a short recess so that they may work out their differences. This usually brings the bickering to a halt, as it is a signal from you that you do not care to listen to it. Once you note your displeasure, the bickering should stop.

77. What should I do if I recognize a witness at the hearing as someone with whom I have had prior contact?

It is possible that you may not recognize the name of a person on the witness list with whom you have had prior contact, and then you recognize the individual, or the individual recognizes you, at the hearing. Also, rebuttal witnesses are usually not listed on the initial witness list, and the first time you are aware of their identity is when they appear to offer testimony.

If you recognize a witness, or a witness recognizes you, immediate disclosure is required. You should inform the parties of your past contact with the witness, and state whether you believe your past contact will affect your impartiality. Obviously, if you think it will, you will withdraw as the arbitrator, even though you are in the middle of a hearing. Usually, immediate disclosure and your statement that your impartiality would not be affected is sufficient for the parties to waive any objection to your past contact with the witness.

78. What is a fact witness?

Most witnesses who testify at an arbitration are fact witnesses. A fact witness is a party or other person who has ***personal knowledge*** of some aspect of the dispute. For instance, in a dispute arising from the collapse of a masonry wall on a construction site during a wind storm, fact witnesses might be the project manager of the contractor, various supervisors and employees who laid the brick, witnesses to the collapse of the wall, and the injured parties. These individuals have personal knowledge as to the nature of the project, the construction of the wall, and the event which is the focal point of the dispute. They were either involved before the collapse in the construction of the wall or were present at its collapse.

While fact witnesses have personal knowledge of the events surrounding the collapse of the wall, they can only testify as to the *facts* they know - e.g., dates, times, individuals involved, construction methods. They usually are not allowed to *opinion* testimony as to the reasons why the events occurred, as it is the duty of the arbitrator to interpret the facts and make inferences from them.

79. What is an expert witness?

In addition to the testimony of fact witnesses, the parties may offer testimony from expert witnesses. An expert witness has no firsthand, personal knowledge of the dispute, but has expertise in the subject matter. While it is the duty of the arbitrator to interpret the facts and make inferences from them, experts offer *opinion* testimony to aid the arbitrator in interpreting the facts.

While most arbitrators do have specific expertise in the subject matter of the dispute, the arbitrator's expertise is not considered a substitute for the use of expert witnesses by the parties to offer opinion as to the interpretation of the facts.

In our previous example of a collapse of a construction wall, the expert witness would render an opinion as to the cause of the collapse. He would do so after reviewing the facts, from documents, statements of witnesses, weather reports, and investigating the site of the collapse. Experts hired by the parties may, and usually do, offer conflicting opinions.

80. How do I know that an expert witness is really an expert?

It is the responsibility of the party presenting the expert to "qualify the expert," i.e. present the qualifications of the expert in the particular subject matter. This is usually done by a review of the expert's resume and having the expert testify concerning his or her expertise in the subject matter. The party for whom the expert is testifying then offers the individual as an expert in the subject matter.

The other party has the right to question the expert as to background and experience and may object to the witness as not having the expertise alleged. The arbitrator also may question the expert as to his or her expertise. It is then the responsibility of the arbitrator to either allow the person to testify as an expert witness or rule that the individual does not have the requisite expertise.

I am often asked how the arbitrator resolves contradictory testimony of expert witnesses if the arbitrator does not have independent expertise in the subject matter. This is a challenge, but you should realize that judges and juries wrestle with contradictory expert testimony in the ordinary course of litigation. I have found that the key to resolving issues of expert testimony is to acquire a basic knowledge in the area of expertise at issue. The goal is not to attempt to replace the experts' expertise with your own, but to gain a basic understanding of the subject matter, even if only the definition of basic terms and concepts.

If you know the key terminology of the subject matter, you can usually ask clarifying questions of experts during or after their testimony. I typically ask more questions of experts than I do of fact witnesses. I try to understand the logic of what they are saying, in the context of the subject matter. In reaching a decision, you need not conclude that one expert is correct while the other expert is wrong. Indeed, you may come to your own understanding based upon the testimony presented.

81. Do I admit a document into evidence that a party has not produced during discovery?

A party who has asked for a document during discovery and has not received it has a reasonable expectation that the information does not exist. If the opposing party presents the information to support its position at the hearing, the party that asked for the document may object, claiming "surprise."

You should not exclude the document, but you should take steps to alleviate the surprise. If the "surprise evidence" is a single document, or only several documents, you may call a brief recess and let the party opposed to admission of the documentation have a chance to review it and prepare questions for cross-examination. If the documents contain a great deal of information, you may not be able to alleviate the surprise by a short recess. You may allow the documents to be introduced and the witness to be examined. Ask the objecting party how much time it would require to review the documentation and prepare cross-examination. It may be that you will require the witness to be recalled for cross-examination several days later, in order to allow sufficient time to prepare for cross-examination.

82. How do the parties summarize what they have proved during the hearing?

There are two methods for summarizing the parties' positions after the testimony is concluded. The parties may make closing arguments or file posthearing briefs. The closing argument is an oral summation of the testimony. A posthearing brief is a written statement that is usually filed several weeks after the conclusion of the hearing. Parties may offer both closing arguments and briefs on specific issues.

83. Should the parties offer closing arguments or posthearing briefs?

Closing arguments may be offered immediately at the conclusion of the testimony or you may recess for several days and reconvene for closing arguments. The parties are given the same amount of time and they may reserve some of their time for rebuttal. For example, each party may have an hour and a half, and the parties may use an hour to present their argument and reserve the last half hour to rebut their opponent's argument.

The purpose of closing arguments is for each party to summarize the significance of the testimony, documentation, and legal positions that have been offered. Request that during closing arguments the parties cite to specific exhibits and testimony to illustrate how they have proved their cases. General statements such as "the documents proved" or "our witnesses proved" are not helpful.

The advantage of closing arguments rather than the submission of written briefs is that the case is ready for decision sooner. The parties will usually ask for at least 30 days to submit briefs. By the time you receive the briefs, the testimony is not as fresh in your memory as it is when closing arguments are offered at the conclusion of the hearing. Unless there is a specific legal issue for which you need additional information, suggest that the parties offer closing arguments. Submission of briefs may add substantially to the cost of the arbitration to the parties, so you should encourage the parties to present the case so that they will conclude the hearing with closing arguments. If the parties insist upon submitting briefs, however, do not discourage their submission. Remember, it is ultimately for the parties to decide how they will present their cases to the arbitrator.

The Arbitration
Award

THE ARBITRATION AWARD

84. How do I decide who prevails?

By the conclusion of the hearing you may have a sense as to which party should prevail, or you may not. You should review your hearing notes and the documentation submitted by the parties, including posthearing briefs. Establish a factual chronology, and let the facts speak for themselves.

Review the arguments of the parties to ascertain if the arguments are supported or contradicted by the facts. Come to conclusions as to credibility of specific witnesses. If you are a member of a three person panel, you should have discussions with your panel members to arrive at a joint decision.

85. How can I make sure I remember what the witnesses look like when I start to deliberate?

This happened to me once, when I gave the parties thirty days to file posthearing briefs. When I began to review my notes, I had no visual impression of one of the witnesses. I now write a brief physical description of the witness in my notes, and try to be as generic as possible. While it is not necessary that you remember the physical appearance of a witness, I find that this memory is helpful to reinforce credibility determinations I have made during the hearing.

You should not write anything unflattering, in case someone inadvertently reads your notes. Sometimes all it takes is the description of an article of clothing to jog your memory - - "red bow tie," etc. By using this type of description, you avoid writing about any physical characteristics of the witness.

86. How can I understand the legal issues if I am not an attorney?

It is the responsibility of the parties and their attorneys to present their position to the arbitrator in a manner that the arbitrator is able to understand. If there is a legal issue that the parties believe is critical to the case, require them to explain it to you, either orally or in writing. If there are court decisions that they believe are applicable, request copies and have the parties highlight or underline the relevant facts and findings. Do not be intimidated. Emphasize to the parties that it is their responsibility to present the case to you. Legal briefs can be submitted before or during the hearing, or as posthearing briefs.

87. When must I render my award?

The rules of most administering organizations specify a period of thirty days from the close of the hearing (after closing arguments or receipt of posthearing briefs) for the arbitrator to consider the evidence and render an award. If the arbitration is not administered by an administering organization, the time period for rendering an award is specified in the parties agreement to arbitrate, or it may be determined by subsequent agreement of the parties or by the arbitrator.

88. What is the format of the award?

The arbitrator's award is not a lengthy document. It states the amount that the claimant and respondent recover on their claims and counterclaims, or that the claim or counterclaim is denied. A date should be specified in the award for interest to commence if the award is not paid by a certain date. The award also designates the party or parties who bear the administrative costs of the arbitration and the arbitrator's compensation. Usually these costs are borne equally. No reasoning is given for the award. **[See Form 4 - Arbitration Award]**

89. What if I am required to write an opinion that includes the reasons for my award?

The arbitration clause in the contract may require a written opinion. You should be aware of this before accepting the appointment as the arbitrator. If there is no contractual requirement for such an opinion, I strongly discourage the parties' request. The arbitrator will spend an excessive amount of time writing a detailed opinion, and the non-prevailing party will have your reasoning to use in an attempt to vacate the award. If there are multiple claims in the arbitration, I suggest to the parties that I render an itemized award, which grants or denies each claim item without further explanation.

If you are required to render a written opinion, you should include in your compensation agreement a clause which stipulates payment for writing the opinion. I include an hourly rate, because I cannot predict the amount of time necessary to write a reasoned opinion.

90. Does the party who does not prevail pay the other party's legal fees?

Usually the parties bear their own legal fees, regardless of who prevails in the lawsuit or arbitration. There are exceptions to the rule. The contract between the parties may state that in the event of litigation or arbitration the non-prevailing party will pay the prevailing party's legal fees. There are also certain laws that allow a prevailing party to recover legal fees under various circumstances. You should be aware that lawsuits and arbitration demands almost always include a request for legal fees. The fact that this request is made does not necessarily mean that there is a basis for awarding legal fees. If a party requests legal fees, you should ask that party to clearly set forth the basis for such request. In addition to explaining the basis for entitlement to legal fees, the party requesting recovery must provide evidence supporting the incurrence and basis of the fee.

After the Award

AFTER THE AWARD

91. When are my duties concluded?

The rendering of the award concludes the duties of the arbitrator. Once you have rendered the award, you have no further responsibility in the matter.

92. What should I do with my notes after I render the award?

Destroy them. There is no advantage whatsoever in keeping your notes, and there is no obligation that you do so. If a suit is filed to vacate the award, a party may subpoena your notes. You cannot produce what does not exist. If you do not destroy them before you receive a subpoena, you cannot destroy them after the subpoena is received.

93. What should I do with the hearing exhibits after I render the award?

It is good practice to return the exhibits to the administering organization or to the parties directly if you have been hired privately. Often the parties do not want them back, but I prefer to return them rather than destroying them or keeping them. If there is a suit to vacate the award, you do not want to have any documentation in your possession that would be responsive to a subpoena, nor do you wish to state that you have destroyed anything which you had received from the parties.

Your best evidence that you have nothing in your possession is a copy of your transmittal letter stating you are returning all copies of exhibits. ***Remember to remove any paper clips or "post-it" notes you may have used to mark documents.***

94. May I discuss my reasoning with the parties after I render the award?

Absolutely not! After you render an award, your responsibility is concluded. You should not, under any circumstances, discuss your reasoning or the basis of your decision with a party or anyone else. You are not required to reveal your reasoning in the award. In revealing your reasoning after the award, the non-prevailing party may find reason to challenge your award. This applies in perpetuity. Do not assume that after several years have passed that it is safe to speak about your reasoning in deciding an arbitration award.

95. How is the arbitration award enforced?

In binding arbitration, the parties have agreed to abide by the arbitrator's decision. Often, the non-prevailing party pays the prevailing party the amount of the award by the date specified, and the matter is concluded.

If the award is not paid, the prevailing party may file a lawsuit to enforce the award. The court reviews the application for enforcement and enters a judgment that can be executed as if it had been rendered by the court. Remember, once you have rendered an award, your duties are concluded. *You should have no interest in, and make no inquiries about, the payment or enforcement of the award.*

96. How does a disappointed party challenge an arbitration award?

Each state has a law which sets forth the grounds for challenging an arbitrator's award. There is also a Uniform Arbitration Act, which most states have adopted, and a Federal Arbitration Act, which governs arbitration arising from agreements involving maritime transactions and interstate commerce.

Typically, the available bases for vacating an arbitrator's award do not involve the substance of the arbitrator's decision, but the ***actions of the arbitrator***. Usually, a court may vacate an award where:

1. The award was procured by corruption, fraud or other undue means.

2. There was evident partiality by an arbitrator.

3. The arbitrators exceeded their powers.

4. The arbitrators refused to postpone the hearing upon sufficient cause being shown or refused to hear evidence material to the controversy or otherwise conducted the hearing so as to substantially prejudice the rights of a party.

It should be emphasized that the fact that the arbitrators may have granted relief that could not or would not be granted by a court is ***not*** a ground for vacating or refusing to confirm an award.

Honest individuals can easily avoid corruption, fraud, and other undue means. However, even the most seasoned arbitrators may place themselves in situations that may later be interpreted as having been partial to one party or another. You must always be cautious before, during, and after the hearing, as well as after rendering the award. Almost every topic discussed in this book involves a pitfall that a disappointed party may attempt to use as a basis for overturning an arbitration award, based on an allegation of partiality.

The best way to safeguard your award is to avoid any possibility of challenge. Admit evidence unless you are absolutely convinced it is neither relevant nor material. Just because you admit evidence does not mean that it was crucial to your decision, or that you relied on it in making to your decision. Treat all parties with respect, keep your distance, and do not put yourself in a position where you are alone at any time with any of the parties or their attorneys.

Payment and Conclusion

PAYMENT

97. How do I arrange compensation for my services?

If you are arbitrating through an administering organization, the organization usually has a range of arbitrator's fees. The parties will agree to compensation within this range, and the case administrator will inform you as to the parties agreement for arbitrator compensation. The administering organization collects the fee from the parties and disburses it to the arbitrator after the award is rendered.

Some organizations offer the first hearing day at no charge for arbitrator's fees, as an incentive to the parties to complete the hearing quickly, and also because arbitrators are to a certain extent considered "volunteers" who are rendering service to the community. Arbitrators, to a point, will volunteer their time in the interest of dispute resolution, but only to a point. Once the hearing extends more than a day, the usual arrangement is to charge a fee for the arbitrator's services. Fees for arbitrations administered through organizations may be hourly or per diem rates. The administering organizations will usually have the arbitrator sign an agreement that the obligation for the payment of the arbitrator's fee is not that of the organization but that of the parties.

For private arbitrations, where the parties contract with the arbitrator directly, the arbitrator has more flexibility in negotiating a fee. Some arbitrators charge an hourly fee, while others negotiate a per diem. Some charge a per diem rate for up to eight hours of hearing time and an hourly rate for hearing time in excess of eight hours in a given day.

You should also arrange for reimbursement for expenses such as travel (transportation and hotel), long-distance phone calls, copying of documents, and any other costs that you incur. I include a provision in my compensation agreement that I may request an advance for travel expenses.

98. How do I make sure I am paid?

As a first step, enter into a written agreement. Administering organizations may have the parties enter into an agreement to deposit the fee in advance of the hearing, and may advise the arbitrator not to proceed with the hearing if the funds are not received.

If you have been retained privately, you should also have a written fee agreement directly with the parties. The agreement should be signed by the parties, and not their attorneys. Require the parties to pay your estimated fees in advance of the hearing.

99. What if one or both parties have not paid in advance when requested?

Render the award during the required time period, sign it, *date it*, and have it notarized. Inform the administering organization, or the parties if you are retained privately, that you have fulfilled your obligation to render the award, and the award is now in your possession. Let them know that as soon as the parties forward full payment to the administering organization, or you, if they have retained you privately, the award will be transmitted. Retain the award in your possession until you are informed by the administering agency that it has received the funds or until you have received the funds from the parties themselves.

I learned my lesson the hard way on this issue. I had a party who *prevailed* in an arbitration refuse to pay my fee. After that, I always make sure that payment is made in advance to the administering organization or to me if the matter is not being administered by an organization.

CONCLUSION

100. What is the most fundamental principle of serving as an arbitrator?

In accepting the position and responsibility of an arbitrator, you place yourself in a situation filled with contention, emotion, and economic distress. The parties look to the arbitrator to control the process. In my early arbitrations, I cautiously exercised my authority, set schedules, ruled on discovery disputes and requests for postponements, and resolved issues that arose during the hearing. The fundamental principle I have learned is simply this:

IF THE ARBITRATOR DOES NOT CONTROL THE PROCESS, FOR THE *BENEFIT* OF ALL CONCERNED, BY FIRMLY EXERCISING AUTHORITY, THE PARTIES WILL CONTROL THE PROCESS, TO THE *DETRIMENT* OF ALL CONCERNED. THEREFORE, BE FAIR, BUT BE FIRM.

101. This is your question

If there is a question that you would like me to answer, please feel free to write, call, or send an e-mail to:

Allan H. Goodman
SOLOMON PUBLICATIONS
POB 2124
Rockville, MD 20847-2124
phone (301)816-1025
book @solomonpublications.com
www.solomonpublications.com

I welcome suggestions and comments.

Forms

FORMS

The following forms may serve as models for use in arbitration proceedings. Remember, if the arbitration is being administered by an organization, you should forward these communications to the case administrator to be sent to the parties, unless the parties have authorized you to communicate directly with them in such instances. If you are administering the arbitration directly, always send copies of the forms to all parties.

Form 1. Request for Preliminary Conference

Dear Case Administrator:

I wish to schedule a preliminary conference in the arbitration between [Claimant] and [Respondent] at my office. At the preliminary conference I request that both the parties and their attorneys attend, so that they may:

1. Provide a brief explanation of the claim [and counterclaim].

2. Agree to a Discovery Schedule for Production of Documents, Responses to Interrogatories, Depositions, and Exchange of Expert Reports.

3. Establish a Schedule for Exchange of Hearing Exhibits, Witness Lists, and Prehearing Briefs.

4. Establish a Hearing Date.

I am available on the following dates. ___ Please forward this letter to the attorneys for the parties, confer with them, and inform me as to the dates that are mutually agreeable for the preliminary conference.

Very truly yours,

Arbitrator

Form 2. Prehearing Order

In the Arbitration Between Claimant and Respondent

PREHEARING ORDER

On ____, a preliminary conference was held in the above matter at [location]. The parties have agreed to the following schedule for further proceedings:

1. Exchange of Requests for Production of Documents and Interrogatories. [date]

2. Last day for submission of Counterclaim by Respondent. [date]

3. Exchange of Documents in Response to Requests for Production, Responses to Interrogatories. [date]

4. Exchange of Expert Reports. [date]

5. Exchange of Exhibits and Witness Lists (Exhibits should be arranged in chronological order to the extent feasible and submitted in tabbed binders. [date]

6. Submission of Prehearing Briefs (5 page limit). [date]

7. Hearing - [date] and continuing until conclusion. Hearing to be held at [location]

8. The parties are advised to request a conference call with the Chairperson of the Arbitration Panel to promptly resolve discovery disputes. The parties should propose three alternate times for the conference call. The Chairperson will contact the other panel members and schedule a conference call.

9. The parties have authorized the Chairperson to execute all subpoenas on behalf of the panel.

_____

Chairperson, Arbitration Panel
[Date]

Form 3. Subpoena

**In the Arbitration between Claimant
and Respondent**

SUBPOENA

TO: Name of Witness
        Address

WE COMMAND YOU, that all business and excuses being laid aside, you and each of you appear and attend before _____, Arbitrator acting under the Arbitration Law of this State, at [location of hearing]

on the ___ day of ___200_, at 10:00 a.m. o'clock to testify and give evidence in a certain Arbitration, then and there to be held between the above entitled parties, and that you bring with you and produce certain documents as listed below:

[list documents requested]

now in your custody.

Requested by: Attorney, [Address, Phone]

_____

                        Arbitrator(s)

Basic Skills for the New Arbitrator

Form 4. Arbitration Award

In the Arbitration Between
Claimant and Respondent

I (we),_____, the arbitrator (s), in this matter, having been sworn and having heard the testimony and other proofs of the parties, AWARD as follows:

Respondent shall pay to Claimant the sum of $_____ due on Claimant's claim against Respondent. [Claimant's claim is denied]

Claimant shall pay to Respondent the sum of $_____ due on Respondent's counterclaim against Claimant. [Respondent's counterclaim is denied]

[Depending on which amount is greater], Claimant [Respondent] shall pay Respondent [Claimant] the balance of $_____, within days of the date of this award, and thereafter to bear interest at the rate of _ % until paid.

The administrative fees and expenses of the [administering organization] shall be paid by [Claimant, Respondent, equally or whatever proportion the arbitrator designates.] The compensation of the arbitrator(s) shall be paid by [Claimant, Respondent, equally or whatever proportion the arbitrator designates.]

THIS AWARD IS IN FULL SETTLEMENT AND SATISFACTION OF ALL CLAIMS AND COUNTERCLAIMS SUBMITTED TO THIS ARBITRATION.

_____
Arbitrator   Date

Solomon Publications offers
the companion volume
BASIC SKILLS FOR THE NEW MEDIATOR

Available from the Publisher and your bookstore.

BASIC SKILLS FOR THE NEW MEDIATOR provides a detailed overview of mediation from the premediation conference through all stages of the mediation session. It guides the new mediator through the mediation process by answering the *one hundred questions most frequently asked* by new mediators. BASIC SKILLS FOR THE NEW MEDIATOR has been used for self-instruction and as a training text. Experienced mediators and attorneys who represent clients in mediation will also find this book extremely useful. The Appendix "Everything You Never Wanted to Know About the Rules of Evidence" is especially valuable for mediators who must deal with the evidentiary vocabulary of the legal profession.

Learn to:
Establish your authority as a mediator
Schedule the mediation session
Deliver the mediator's opening statement
Prioritize issues
Preside during joint sessions
Conduct private caucuses
Overcome impasses
Identify "hidden agenda" and "throwaway" items
Deal with parties who lack settlement authority
Aid parties to achieve a viable settlement

"A methodical introduction that provides a detailed outline of what to expect, what to plan for, and possible flash points."

National Institute for Dispute Resolution News, April 1997.

SOLOMON PUBLICATIONS PO Box 2124 Rockville, Maryland 20847
phone (301) 816-1025
book@solomonpublications.com
www.solomonpublications.com